Discourse on Human Freedom

The Chronicles of a Survivalist

Ben Wood Johnson, Ph.D.

TESKO

Middletown, Pennsylvania

Johnson, Ben Wood

Discourse on Human Freedom / Ben Wood Johnson. — Tesko Publishing ed.

ISBN-13: 978-1-948600-31-6 (pbk.)

ISBN-10: 1-948600-31-5

This book was first published in September 2020

The information illustrated in this book was compiled for a school project.
The analysis is based on class notes and other materials.

Johnson, Ben Wood

Discourse on Human Freedom

Tesko Publishing website address: www.teskopublishing.com

Tesko Publishing/Eduka Solutions
330 W. Main St. #214
Middletown, PA 17057, USA

Printed in the United States of America

Cover Illustration Wood Oliver

To freedom lovers all over the world

Contents

Contents

Prologue

To be free is to be without restraints. To be without manacles [be they in the mind or in the flesh] is to be independent of anything that is [or everything that might be]. But that state of being is nearly impossible. It is therefore well within the realm of logic to conclude that no living being is free, at least, not on this planet. Yet, most people believe they are free. What might explain such a worldview?

This work explores, although it does so briefly here, the intellection of freedom. It is a reflection about the notion of liberty (or self-determination) within a particular context. The goal is to put a spotlight on the issues.

I started writing this book many years ago. But I was sidetracked by other projects. In the light of the coronavirus outbreak, the line between individual independence to be the way that he or she might please at any given point in time and the right of the collective to override individual rights became blurry. I realized that arguments outlining the importance of individual freedom were absent in the debate. I decided to revisit the subject.

The book does not explain abstract concepts. The purpose is to explore the degree to which human beings are free. Another goal, although it is utterly echoed throughout the manuscript, is to sketch out whether a person could be free unconditionally or whether he could be sans restrictions in the world.

The text taxes the obstacles that might impede human freedom. But the book does not entertain inescapable conclusions about the concept. Despite its limits, this work is not a fruitless intellectual pursuit. It was designed to entertain your curiosity.

The book offers a practical approach about human freedom. It offers real-world examples to clarify the viewpoints that permeate the current debate. Perhaps the views echoed throughout the text will help you make sense of the literature.

The intimation commonly known as freedom is not a controversial issue. For the most part, there is no disagreement in the literature. But this word offers a contrasting opinion.

The text includes eighteen chapters. While these sections are not lengthy, they are coherent; they are succinct. Moreover, the book contains intuitive comments about the conjecture of free will and choice.

The book is in the form of a long essay. But the analysis outlined in the document is not the result of an empirical observation. Rather, this work was inspired by several lived experiences. All the same, the observations highlighted throughout the text emanated from an immigrant's perspective.

In sum, this collection of essays is undersized; that is, considering the complex nature of the topic. Notwithstanding, the text does not look at complex philosophical questions. But do not let that deter you from enjoying this anthology. This is a great intellectual piece. In that spirit, I encourage you to immerse yourself in the document as thoroughly as possible.

Good Reading!

Ben Wood Johnson, Ph.D.

May 2020

Introduction

There is no dearth of writings about human freedom. You would be hard pressed not to find a book in your library, which talks about freedom. Of course, some of those writings might have a political slant. Nonetheless, you certainly have an idea about how scholars, thinkers, or philosophers (be they contemporary or else) talk about human freedom.

Despite our insights about freedom, we have no clue as to what it truly entails. This is to say, what we know about the phenomenon is patently wrong. For these reasons, what we understand to be freedom is anything but that.

Discourse on Human Freedom

Freedom, I will echo here, is elusive; it is a gimmick; it is a fallacy; it is a feel good consideration, which may have no real utility for our continued survival in our treacherous journey in this world; that is, unless we understand the need to be free in its most fundamental sense.

On this stone called earth, there is no freedom to be had. That being noted, there exists panoply of ways to construe a similar state of being. That construal may become a determinant factor for our long-term existence.

Some of you may disagree with the views I will echo throughout the manuscript. Granted, I offer a peculiar viewpoint about the conceit of freedom. I reckon that my position might not be in unanimity. With a bit of luck though, I hope to change your mind as you thumb through the document.

If you are still reading this brief introduction, perhaps you are open to a new approach in the debate. Perhaps you are curious about what I will say. In any case, I encourage you to remain open-minded in your assessment of this work.

Most people would argue that freedom is real. Some would even say that they are always free to be however and whenever they want. Freedom, from their vantage point, is an easily attainable state. Freedom, from a narrow perspective, is always achievable. Freedom, from that worldview, is at all times sustainable. Withal, these views are flawed. These approaches are misguided.

Freedom is a useless passion. It is real to the extent you want it to be. It is ephemeral or perhaps it is unreal to the extent others want it to be that way. Thus, you are neither free nor you could ever be that way.

Your freedom is always intangible. Your liberty is a myth. Your so-called "free will," your supposed sense of self, or even your make belief "self-determination" is not of this world. All you have is the perception of being free, which, in and of itself, could never be real in the most tangible sense. Thereafter, freedom, if any sense of it you were to possess, would always be relative to your capacity to imagine yourself to be that way.

Discourse on Human Freedom

Not considering of popular assumptions about the notion of freedom, I will take a different approach in the debate. In spite of popular accounts about the concept, I offer a singular viewpoint here. Certainly, most people believe they are free. But I will argue to the contrary in this diatribe. If you would like to learn more, join me in this literary adventure...

1

Freedom as a Fallacy

The intuition of freedom, at least, the manner in which most people understand it, results from an erroneous belief. It is, to say the least, a falsehood. The way a person envisions his freedom is always unreal. Thus, the concept of human freedom is an illusion in any way imaginable. This is so, I would echo, in any manner conceivable.

Human beings concoct freedom as a mechanism to bare their existence in a world devoid of meaning. As well, freedom reflects human beings' perception of their reality. But that view, in and of itself, is not necessarily a representation of verity in its most tangible form.

The actuality that human beings perceive as a state of being free is antithetic to the postulation of freedom itself. Humanity was not designed to be free. Nature does not [or could not] allow human beings to be free. Thinking that we are free is a way to deal with our perpetual state of bondage. We will never be free so long as we are grounded on earth.

While we may think that we are free, we also know [or perhaps we understand as well] that we will never enjoy anything resembling freedom in the true sense of the term. But that deduction often creates a sense of fallibility in us. This truth often exacerbates our sense of precocity in a world designed to extirpate our existence from it anytime. Striving for freedom, more often than not, is an escape route, which would allow us to deny our social reality. It is generally a pursuit in futility.

The more we crave for freedom, the more we enslave ourselves in the name of it. The more we seek freedom, the more we deny our nature as a result. But the more we deny our naturality, the farther away we would like to dwell from it. The tragedy is that the farthest away we claim to be from our nature, the closer we get to it. We strive to refute an absoluteness, which will never go away. Freedom is unattainable for other reasons. For instance, we could never be free; that is, so long as we evolve in the natural. Even in the abstract, we will never be free; that is, so long as we evolve in a social arrangement. Yet, most people believe they are free. Why there is such an incongruity in the verisimilitude human beings generally face [or even what they perceive] every day of their lives?

I could not put in plain words the rationale a person might give the self for perceiving the self to be free, even though that might not be the case in any way, shape, or form. I could not deduce how individuals make out their freedom or the lack of that. There is a need to examine, even though I do not do so exhaustively in this instance, the degree to which human beings are free.

The human materiality (be it natural, social, or else) is demoralizing. Most assuredly, we are conscious of that crusade. But we have to deal with that actuality, even when we might be incapable of doing so.

We live in a coercive [if not, a contrived] world. Everything we do in that milieu [or everything we omit from doing in it] is required of us; it may be demanded from us as a prerequisite so we could be.

Sometimes our nature demands that we exist a certain way. Other times, we obligate ourselves to exist in a particular way. At all time and in every way possible [or even any manner imaginable by the human mind], we are under control. That everlasting state of bondage makes it impossible for us to exist on our own. It makes it improbable for us to be beyond chance.

We invent a coping mechanism to deal with our constant desire to be free from our natural emprises. But this is a pointless pursuit. And so, we invent an apparatus to accept our lack of freedom. We lie to ourselves.

Human beings are not free. However farfetched this view might seem to some, it holds true in the most trivial sense. Freedom is a feel good notion, which carries no tangible truth. As a result, human beings are not free and could never be that way in any way, shape, or form. Put simply, a person could never be free, at least, not on this planet. What might explain the reason for that reality? The most obvious truth is that we do not hold the capacity to be free. We were not designed to be that way.

For us [human beings] to be free, we would have to be disconnected from the natural. We would have to be without wires, which would be paradoxical in nature, for we were conceived out of the natural. Our nature is tied up with the natural. But we could only exist within the natural.

To be free, at least, as human beings tend to conceive that state of being, we would have to hold God-like features. But to achieve freedom from the self or from the natural, we would have to possess unworldly traits. To be precise, we would have to hold alien attributes. We would have to possess extraterrestrial abilities.

Since human beings possess none of the features previously noted, we could never be free. We could never be devoid of ourselves. We could never be outside the realm of the natural.

Freedom, at least, as human beings perceive it, is a chimera. It is a figment of our imagination. We could never be that way, at least, not on earth. We could never be free in a world designed to capture our beingness whenever it pleases. We hold no tangible grip over our destiny, although we tend to think that we do.

It is irrefutable that human beings matter to a certain degree within the natural. As such, we are a part of the natural itself. We make of our world what it is. But we could only carve the world to the extent that the world would allow us to carve it.

We are part of both our good and bad fortunes in a milieu, which we did not construe or could not rearrange. Regardless of our reality, we belong to the natural. We are enshrined in our nature. We are dependent of our nature. The natural and *us* [human beings] (i.e., we…) are the same.

The world is not an exogenous entity. There, everything functions in unison. In the scenery where human beings evolve, every entity is part of a whole. That whole is a part of a multitude. That multitude, in turn, forms the entity, which we know as planet earth. Thus, in the most tangible sense, no living entity could be free from the grip of the natural terrain. This is the essence of our destiny.

On earth, we are supposed to be ordinary men. We are supposed to be human beings. We were not designed to be super men. We are not supposed to be super humans.

In making the previous assertions, I would admit that deciphering the term freedom is not that simple. It is not that easy to elucidate this concept. Similarly, this book does not hold the ultimate truth on the matter. Granted, it could be difficult to explicate the nature of human freedom objectively, for this work reflects my own biases and my own preconceived notions about the subject.

The concept of freedom is exceptionally subjective. Views about the notion can be ideological or even political. I could not speak on behalf of humanity in this work. Despite that undeniable realization, I hope to examine presumptions about human freedom from a philosophical slant.

2

Confinement and Freedom

Between 2019 and 2020, a major pandemic engulfed the world. It was the coronavirus (also known as the Covid-19). This illness revealed human flaws in the most shocking manner. It diluted our perceived greatness over the natural.

Overnight, millions fell ill. In a short period as well, millions more perished under the ferocious grip of the malady. It was surreal for most people. The virus wreaked havoc in various countries. It was blatant; it was violent.

For a brief interlude, humanity had to learn to accept the unpleasant truth of their inconsequential nature within the natural. They had to come to their senses in relation to their perpetual precocity on a planet designed to consume every part of their being. Human beings had to concede defeat. They had to surrender to the virus.

Many people realized their fragility in a hood, about which they knew little. They realized that they knew absolutely nothing about their selves in the natural. Before the rapid expansion of the illness, there was no solution in sight. World governments were caught off guard. Even our so-called scientists could not pipe any words, which could reassure us that everything was going to be all right.

Most modern societies were on their knees. The so-called "developed nations" were begging for mercy. Some resorted to piracy on the high seas to secure their survival, which they considered in peril. They stooped down to a height never seen before in the annals of history. The panic reached a point never imagined, at least, not in modern times.

Many world leaders appealed to God. Others relied on providence for an exemption of some sort. Some recoiled on their technologies, thinking they would find the ultimate panacea to cure the disease. There as well, there was no hope. Many found out that the best technologies human beings had to offer were useless before the ferocity of the virulent malady.

During the pandemic, the chasm between rich and poor became petty. The ability for some people to live in comfort, while others dwelt in abject poverty, became super flux. The rift between the haves and the have-nots became immaterial.

Those who, for years, claimed to be inheritors of super humans found out this was not the case at all. They found out, in the most vexing ways of course, that life, at least, as they have always known it, is not relative to a person's degree of wealth, social status, religious affiliations, or even country of origin. They found out that they were in the same boat [so to speak] with everyone else. It became evident that we, as a species, were experiencing the same sordid adventure on an unsegregated planet.

During the pandemic as well, we found out that our so-called modern hospitals were ill equipped to deal with age-old diseases and mundane illnesses, which the natural generally provides the necessary ingredients to cure swiftly and well. We were not prepared to deal with nature in its most intrinsic state. Contrary to what we had been saying to ourselves, we had not mastered the natural after all.

Our so-called "best doctors" were overwhelmed by the sheer viciousness of the disease. Healthcare workers could not address the needs of the population, which they were supposed to serve. Even they needed help. Oh, it was a mess.

During the climax of the deadly epidemic, it became obvious that modern medicine was a publicity stunt, for it could not provide any tangible answer, which could help us address the dire situation that humanity had been facing. Before the absolute brute force of the natural (Mother Nature, as it were), the scientific community was in limbo. All they could do was to hide from the wrath of the disease like anyone else.

Nobody had answers. No one knew what was going on. No one knew what to do to assuage the pain and the suffering that plagued the planet. It was a guessing game.

Humanity, I would go as far to say, was left to fend for itself. It was a heaven for charlatans; it was a feast for social scavengers; it was a wonderful opportunity for political predators and the like to further misguided political ideologies. Demagogues held a place of honor during these times of horror.

Many people sought to benefit from the crisis as much as they could. Some even helped concoct policies, which they claimed would help reduce, if not, to stop, the propagation of the malady. In spite of it all, the number of people that died from the virus continued to rise. Of course, many more recovered.

Perhaps in response to the hysteria and the hype, which had been built up about the disease, world leaders sought to regain control of the situation. Out of fear, out of bad faith, or perhaps out of ignorance, governments around the globe adopted stringent measures. They said such actions were necessary to curb the spread of the virus.

In spite of efforts undertaken to stop the illness, new cases swelled like a wild fire. The virus was everywhere. No country was exempted. No social class was spared. No social caste system was off the hook. It was the closest humanity got to a full-blown cataclysm, at least, in recent memory.

In the midst of the global health crisis brought on by the coronavirus outbreak, a lot happened to the population of the world. There was a massive assault against individual freedom. In the name of protecting the collective (or in the name of protecting society), there was a blatant disregard for human rights. It was as if human civilization had been retrograded to the stone ages.

Leaders around the globe (largely, ill-fronted authorities) decided, most often unilaterally, what they thought were good practices for the collective. They decided which conduct was apt, if not necessary, for the individual. They invaded the person in his core being. Several entities, some might say, reached a status of eminence in society. Some awarded themselves the status of God or they pretended to be that way.

During that period, which, some observers might argue, is still a part of our new reality, privacy mattered less. Individual freedom, in many cases, vanished. The right to be on their person, which most people thought they enjoyed, also vanished in the thin air.

Countries enacted lockdown policies, which required the individual to stay at home. In most authoritarian places, there were curfews. The police were out patrolling the streets with batons and all sorts of devices contrived specifically to intimidate people. The sheer brute force of States to enforce their authority was visible for all to see.

Most countries imposed draconian policies, such as wearing facemasks. Authorities enforced capricious social rules with the degree of callousness that would only make sense in a dystopian world or in a nightmare. Those who were infected by the virus were placed in quarantine. Those suspected of being infected were also put aside. There was a general sense of fear across many lands.

While some states enforced those policies in the most civilized manner, others were unhinged. The Internet was filled with images [or videos] of police beating people up for not wearing facemasks or for not wearing their masks the appropriate manner [or properly]. There were instances where people, most often grown men and women, were being told how to be, where to be, and when to be.

Some people received penalties [or fines] for disobeying established rules. Others were assaulted by law enforcement officials for not abiding by social distancing rules. Some were even arrested for protesting the new rules. It was complete madness.

As I witnessed this lunacy, I pondered about the state of freedom. Then, it hits me. There is no freedom in this world. We are all in some sort of a cage. For sure, some of us are more restricted than others are. Whatever the case might be, we are [all] in this labyrinth together.

3

Examining the Term Freedom

E very human being must survive. So long as it is within his capabilities to do so, a person must find a way to prolong his existence in the turf where he evolves. The individual must struggle to find his way, although achieving this task might not be always possible. Realizing this feat might not be always propitious. Concretizing this aim might not even be feasible.

No matter what, the person must strive to survive.[1] Emphatically, he might have to do so at all costs and by any means necessary. A central

---

[1] See the book titled *Striving to Survive* to learn more about this notion.

hindrance to human survival is the absence [or the lack of] freedom. Human beings are not free to the extent that we would like it to be. We evolve in a world of seclusion. We live in a state of restraint.

What does the term human freedom imply? This is an interesting question. To be honest, I do not know what it means to be free, for I have never been at that state.

I am not the only one who has never experienced true freedom though. No human being has ever been free. To be free is to be outside the scope of nature. But no living entity within the natural could make such a claim. No living entity has ever been free, although such a pursuit is vital for existence.

Apart from the previous arguments, the common belief is that human beings are free. Otherwise, they always enjoy such a capacity. I am not sure this view is accurate. At most, I would argue that this is not the case in every instance.

As a human being, I know that I am not free. But I could be intransigent. I could indulge in bad faith. I could lie to myself. I could say to myself that I am free. I could make myself believe that I am that way. Of course, that would not make it so in the most tangible sense.

In spite of being aware of my reality, I might not recognize (or even acknowledge) that actuality as a veracity. I might deny my own needs to further that of others. I might be lost in my isolation. I would also be dwelling in bad faith. I would view my world [or the world that others experience, for that matter] from a misguided sagacity.

In this analysis, brief though it is [or however trivial it might appear to some observers], the goal is to look at the term freedom. In this instance—of course—I hope to do so as concisely as possible. Another goal—worthy of note here—is to reflect on the tour de force human beings face in their stomping ground.

My scrutiny of the term freedom is not necessarily a means to vent. It is not a ploy on my part to echo my own frustrations. It is not a strategy to deny my own happening in my social milieu.

Rather, this work is an ontological assessment of human realities in places where such conjectures could be in disguise. It is important to assess, though in a few words here, the plight for human survival and the grounds on which a person might want to do so. It is crucial to discuss the issues a person might face during his search for freedom, even though such a quest could be in vain.

Another constituent (or perhaps a unique impediment) to human freedom, which is also worth outlining here, is immigration. There is a link between human survival and human freedom. And so, a parallel between survival and immigration is worthy of further scrutiny. The person might feel constrained in a foreign social *mise en scène*. He might abandon the search for freedom altogether.

The mindset of freedom is a subjective construct of our experience. It is a reaction to our ineluctable discovery of our brutal reality. It is a way for us to deny that actuality. For this reason, the term freedom, at least, the way we [human beings] concretize it, is whimsical at its core meaning.

What is freedom for one person is not necessarily the same for another. One is free (or a person may feel that way) so long as there is no one else who could snatch that freedom (or that perception) away from the individual. Then, for us human beings, the line between being free and dwelling in captivity is as thin as our capacity to conceptualize our quiddity in the world.

To put the previous idea in context, let us say that understandings about the concept of freedom may depend on how a person perceives his quintessence at a given point in time. It may be the result of a deep analysis of the self. It may also reflect how a person views the self in relation to others in a social milieu.

Ideas about the notion of freedom may stem from personal opinions. They may be the results of a person's worldview. They may emanate from the individual's own experience in the place where he evolves. But what could be considered freedom could as well be described as the lack of that. Let us explore this theory further to make sense of it all.

Discourse on Human Freedom

4

Views about Human Freedom

If we were to analyze the term freedom in its intrinsic sense, it would be impossible to come to terms with the true meaning of the hypothesis. It would be useless to rely on personal experiences to show what the term means in a tangible sense. What is freedom then?

At first blush, one could say that freedom is a feel-good persuasion. Human beings invented it to make sense of their essence. Freedom, if it existed at all, would be indiscernible. If not, it would be unrecognizable, at least, with the naked eye.

Considering the subjective nature of the theorem, we would never come to a consensus about what the term truly entails. In other words, there is no objective precept, which we could use to examine this axiom. There is no patented way of looking at the subject. This is a complex issue, I must admit.

Examining the fancy of freedom is a daunting task. In this short compilation as well, I do not [or I could not] look at the perspicacity of the acuity of the notion of being free in depth. The concept is foreign to the natural. Freedom, at least, as a tangible state of being, is not of this world.

Being free is to be outside the norms of being in the natural. To be free is to be independent of everything and anything. To be free is to be a superman or a creature from outer space.

Being free is to be outside any constraint, which is exogenous to our nature. Being free is to be beyond everything. Be that as it may, in our present living arrangements [I must also point out] this is not possible. Within the natural habitat itself, every living being must rely on the existence [or the person] of another.

That irrefutable factuality entails an inescapable dependence on the natural. A person could not be free from the natural. One could not be free, for one's existence is intrinsically intertwined with that of others. Granted, this is a peculiar viewpoint about human freedom. But there is more to the concept than most people realize.

In this book, I could take a common approach to the conjecture of freedom. I could echo, as so many others have done it, that we are free. I could proclaim that every human being can be free. From the start though, I would have to sway myself of that ill-conceived verity, which I could not do in all honesty here.

I could evoke cryptic jargons to clarify the wit of freedom. I could reference works by well-known thinkers to support my views. I could put on display my academic skills. I could highlight my made out intellectual prowess. I could echo my expertness [or my dexterity] to decipher difficult philosophical notions. I could exhibit my capacity to relay theoretical principles. But the present opus is not such a work.

Discourse on Human Freedom

What might be incontestable is that the social scheme where we find ourselves is an impediment for freedom. Being in a confined surrounding is the opposite of being free. Society is a confined jungle. In such a climate, the collective holds an unprecedented control over the individual. To say it again, so long as we evolve in a social hub, we could never be free.

There is a need to examine the nature of the grip society holds on human beings. We must consider the effects of that possession. There is a need to explore obstacles, which could be harmful to a person. There is a need to examine the danger the collective poses for the individual [or for individual freedom] in its most prosaic sense. Let us grasp understandings about human freedom further.

5

The State of Being Free

Being free is *he* who decides *when* to be, *how* to be, *what* to be, and *why* to be.[2] Being free is to be without restraints. Being free is to be without restrictions.

Outside the reach of the natural, achieving freedom is an impressive feat. Nonetheless, no human being has ever been free in nature. Within the natural as well, assumptions about freedom are not that complicated to grasp. There can be a bit of tangibility to the presupposition.

---

[2] No human beings enjoy the capacity to be according to his [own] accord. Every being can only be when others are.

Being free is not always a sensory perception of the state of being itself. It can be real; it can be factual; that is, this is so to the extent that the being who perceives such a freedom also understands the implication of the state thereof. The being must be able to perceive the self in a state of being free in relation to other beings, be they tangible or else.

If I were able to go wherever I please at any given point in time, I might surmise that I am free. I could make out that I am able to go wherever I want and I could do so at any given time. My freedom would appear tangible to a point where I might construe it to be real or even unadulterated.

In the real world, however, this is not the case at all. In fact, anywhere that we find ourselves, we are more constrained than we are free. We are more restricted than we realize. We are more under control than we could fathom.

In our current state of bondage, we are slaves both in the mind and in the flesh. But we are inclined to think that we are free. Most people genuinely believe that they are free. Others endeavor relentlessly to emancipate themselves.

What might explain that reality? Should I say, what might explain our incapacity to grasp our own verity?

When we [humans] speak of freedom, we are likely to limit ourselves to a mere state of being. It is the state of being free. We are likely to content ourselves to a simple *état d'être*, which embodies our perception of what freedom is or what it could be. Excluding, if we were to tell the truth to ourselves and to others, we would have to admit there is more to freedom than a mere state of the mind at a particular point in time. There is more to freedom than a perception; there is more to liberty than even a construed state of being.

Human freedom, if it existed at all, would always be ephemeral. The theory itself indicates a state of being that is more complex than a mere ability to be within a unique social topography. Freedom is a state of being, which is devoid of any tangibility. It is beyond our current state of physical restraint.

Being free is to be beyond one's Beingness. Being free is to be beyond nature. Hence, freedom must be a state of transcendence within the natural elements where men evolve.

Human freedom, to reiterate, is both a perception and a tangible state of being. Freedom is a perception because it is the result of a subjective introspection. It is tangible because, being about to perceive that one is free could make a world of a difference in the way a person might perceive his existence in the most trivial sense.

By contrast, not being able to perceive freedom could have a detrimental effect on the person. Thus, perceiving one's freedom or concretizing the lack of it could have real world consequences, which the person might not be able to navigate on his own or for his own. The incongruity is that the tangible nature of freedom—in and of itself—is illusory. If not, that tangibility results from the perception of being free itself. It is a vicious circle. One is free so long as one wants to be that way. But wanting to be free is no guarantee of achieving that state of being.

Freedom is, at least, to most people, the capacity to exert movements. That is, one is free so long as one can go from one location to another. But this state of being is not necessarily a sign of freedom.

Being able to move about is not an embodiment of freedom. Even if you were put in a cage, so long as the cage is not tightly spaced out, you would still be able to move about. Yet, being in a cage, in any way, shape, or form is not an indication of freedom, at least, if we were to examine the concept from a metaphysical lens.

As a perception, freedom must be envisioned in the mind before it could be concretized in the flesh. If you could not imagine being free, then you could not be free. If you could not construe your freedom a certain way, you could not imagine it in any way. This is the nature of human realities in the real world when it comes to their quest for freedom.

Although that state of being is always transient, we tend to assimilate it to being free. Any other way, there must be more to freedom than a mere ability to exert muscular functions. There must be more to freedom than a want to be free or a mere desire to be that way.

The freedom itself must be intrinsic. It must be elemental to the person. Being free must mean being without restraints or being devoid of limits. So long as your *freedom* comes from this or from that, you are not free. So long as some entity decides whether you are free or whether you could be free, then you could never be free. This is the extent of the present intellectual tête-à-tête.

Let me ask you once more. What is freedom in an intrinsic sense then? Are you free? Better yet, do you believe that you are free? If you believe that you are free, what makes you certain that you are indeed free?

If I were to tell you that you are not free, would you believe me. Would you equate my assessment of your state of being inconsequential to your real state of being? Would you refute me? Would you offer evidence to support your belief that you are in fact free?

Imagine that I demand you to prove that you are free, how would you respond? What if I said that you could never be free, would my assertion make sense to you? Would you ask me to go away?

Would you disavow me? Would you enlighten me about what freedom is and why it is necessary?

What if I am an illegal immigrant, do you think that the term freedom would mean the same to you as it does to me? Do you think I could enjoy freedom? Would you try to convince me that I could be free just as you are or just as you perceive yourself to be?

Perhaps these are vague questions. They may not even make sense to you, especially if you are not a person living under a constant fear of losing any sense of freedom. Perhaps you never experienced such a state of being. Even if any of the above understandings were to apply to you, the vagary of the term freedom, at least, the way I understand it, might still make no sense to you. This is the subjective nature of the concept.

To reiterate, there is an irrefutable link between immigration and freedom. People who live in a foreign social atmosphere may find it hard to feel free. If the environment does not create an atmosphere to make the person feel safe, he might never feel free.

Freedom is, on the outset, a mental outlook. One is free so long as one thinks that way. One is free so long as one feels that way. But most people have a romantic view of what freedom is or what it could be. In truth, there is more to the delusion about freedom than meets the eye. I will reiterate a similar viewpoint in the remaining portion of the text.

6

The Fantasy of Freedom

Freedom [or the illusion thereof] is a frame of mind. Then again, the concept is always the result of a subjective viewpoint. It is not a concrete state of being in and of itself. Freedom is a transient way of being at a particular point in time. Thus, one is free so long as one has the capacity, the ability, or the disposition to feel that way at a given point.

While the fantasy of freedom reflects a human set up, it has real consequences. Even though the concept is the result of a person's construal of the reality around him, the reasoning, to say it again, has practical implications, which go far beyond the capacity of the human mind to comprehend. In certain instances, perceptions about freedom or the lack of that can be tangible; they can be palpable. Therefore, to most people, being free or not being able to enjoy any sense of freedom could be as real as it could get.

Being deprived of freedom or a similar illusion could also be as tangible as it could ever be. For instance, the person could be in jail. He could be forced to live under conditions that might limit his movements. His whereabouts or his way of being could be under constant scrutiny.

I do not know where the reverie about freedom emanated. Despite the obvious mismatch in the way that we are likely to perceive the term, a universal reality about the concept could be hard, if not impossible, to rebuke. We long for freedom. That yearning is also the essence of our existence.

Human beings seek freedom from everything within the natural. We are connected with anything that exists. To echo a previous statement, we are wired with the natural. We are a part of nature. As such, we could not detach ourselves from it. We are the prisoners of our own existence.

That actuality might explain the reason we [human beings] often feel the need to be free. This state of being is even more depressing when we evolve in a social encompassment. Under a similar regimen, we live under sets of rules that often undermine our nature.

When a person finds out that he must live under conditions that are foreign to his nature, that individual would also live in a state of bondage. That state of repression or that instance of oppression could be mental; it could be physical; it could be political; it could be economic. Under such a circumstance, the person would not be living as his nature intended. The intrinsic want to be free or the innate desire to be as one's nature intended would become an alibi, which the person might provide the self for longing for freedom.

Every time a person lives in a situation of unnatural restrictions, he would ineluctably uncover that he must be free. Every time a person finds the self in a situation of restraint in his core being, he would invariably develop a natural thirst for freedom. That individual would always seek to emancipate the self from the state of reclusion that he finds the self, which may or may not be real.

No matter what, the individual would seek to rid the self of any real or any perceived state of bondage. The problem is that these efforts are seldom fruitful. Therefore, the man lives in a state of unnatural restrictions, some of which are his own doing. Other restraints might be foreign to the person's nature. The same, the man is always under the purview of others. Nonetheless, the person may think that he is under his own governing.

When a person thinks that he is free, this belief may become engrained in his psyche. He may not be able to perceive the cage, which can be mental, physical, or both, where he finds the self. This is the tragedy of the intangibility of freedom.

A man's world is filled with all types of constraints. In such a world, there is no real freedom to be had. It is a world of restraint. Every facet of a man's existence depends on the existence of another. Thus, a man is free [or he may perceive such a state of being] only when others make that freedom [or such a perception] possible.

Ben Wood Johnson

We are the prisoners of our time. We are so long as others are not. We are so long as others are according to our expectations. Sometimes, we are so long as others would allow us to be.

To be clear, I am not trying to dismiss the term freedom [or the need of that]. Instead, I hope to reveal the mythical facets of this incubus. I do not think the need for freedom is a pretentious desire. Wanting freedom is as natural as wanting to grow wings and to fly. The problem is that being able to fly is not necessarily a human thing.

Human beings were not designed to spread their wings and fly away. Any human desire to fly must be the result of a passion and not necessarily because of a prerequisite to further one's existence. That desire, regardless of its origins or not considering its consequences, must be transient at its core. Thus, a human's desire to fly is always going to be aberrant, even though the person might concoct the appropriate means to become airborne at some point in time.

For the sake of the argument, let us say that human beings can fly. What would that feat implicate? Would that suggest human freedom in its most natural state?

A plausible answer is that being able to fly would be unnatural. Otherwise, it would not fall outside the limits the natural entourage imposes on human beings. Simply put, human beings are not supposed to fly. Any means that would allow human beings to fly would ineluctably put them outside the scope of the natural. Thus, such a reality could only be an ephemeral state of being, for it would be perverted.

Anything that was born out of the natural could only be [that is, it could only exist] within the natural. Nothing that came from the artificial could ever become natural. The scope of human freedom, coincidentally, falls within the latter category. To that extent, freedom [or the need thereof] is always outside of the natural itself. As such, it is always the result of a false impression of the milieu. That is the rationalization, I would argue, which could provide us a few details as to why freedom would always be unattainable, at least, in the tangible realm.

7

Wanting Freedom

Why would not I want freedom? Why would not you want to be free? Why would it not make sense to want to emancipate oneself from a reality of dependence that one finds the self whether it is natural, artificial, societal)?

Any answer to the preceding inquiries would reveal the mental state of the person answering these questions in the most banal sense. Granted, most people would answer yes to the previous queries, even if they might not fully grasp (or even comprehend) the implications of such a state of being. Whether we look at freedom from a natural monocle or whether we see it from a societal optic,

Discourse on Human Freedom

every living being wants freedom or the illusion of that state of being. Intrinsically speaking, we [that is, human beings] would like to be free. But this is not where the issue lies for me.

When we speak of freedom, we romanticize our natural state. We imagine a world empty of the natural. Freedom, to us, is transcendence. Freedom, from our vantage point, is beyond our nature. Freedom, by that logic, is a state of superhuman.

There are no tangible ways of achieving a state of independency, which would extract us from nature. There is no way to be outside the confine of the natural milieu. We could never be free so long as we are human. Therefore, the freedom that we crave so much will never come true.

Human beings must depend on X or Y. They must be under the scope of one entity or they must be [or they must evolve] under the guide of another. Human beings were born out of the natural. They belong [only] in that milieu. As such, human beings could never be free outside the natural. This factuality is one facet of freedom or the lack of that, which we have yet to accept.

For a good portion of our existence, we have been lying to ourselves. We are convinced that the mere fact that we can be in the natural in ways, which other living entities are not (or could never be, at least, from our vantage point), this is an indication that we are free. But this view is inaccurate. It is based on a misguided introspection of ourselves in the natural environs.

Freedom, if any glimpse of it were to exist out there, would be illusory, if not, it would be invisible to the naked eye. It would only be perceptible with the mind. Hence, real freedom would [or could] only exist in the abstract.

In echoing the previous contentions, a synthetic approach to the concept of freedom is worthy of note in this discourse. From a human attitude, freedom is a wonderful state of the mind. It is a pleasant state of being, which, most often, has little or nothing to do with the real world that the person experiences in his quotidian. Under other conditions, being free [or feeling that way] could have undeniable implications, which could also distort a person's sense of self in the world.

Perceptions about freedom could influence how a person comports the self. It could further the individuals sense of self. It could render precarious a person's existence. It could also undermine that existence to a point of annihilation.

If we could examine the whim of freedom as authentically as possible, we might be able to learn to accept the nature of our world. We might learn to become attuned to the factualness of our social environment. We might learn our place in the world. We might learn to strive to protect the self in a perfidious terrain. We might learn to strive to survive in the milieu itself.

When it comes to freedom or the lack of that, there is a brutal reality, which we must learn to accept. In this instance, we live in a co-dependent world. As a result, our perception about freedom or the lack of that is relative to how others perceive our Beingness. It may also be the result of how we perceive our own Beingness in relation to that of others. In it lies the dichotomy of wanting freedom and being afforded albeit in a capricious manner, such a possibility.

8

Depending on the Other

Every facet of Beingness—this is not necessarily or this is not exclusively that of human beings—is based on that of another entity's state of being. We are human beings. We are a part of a multitude. We are a constituent of the human species. Our Beingness depends on that of another.

Human beings are not free. We could never be that way, at least, not in a world of constraints. For that reason, human beings could never be free. Strictly speaking, we could never be free from our own encroachments.

The tragedy of our existence reflects our tendency to undermine one another. For us to survive, we must seize others. We must also make sure that others do not (or could not) seize us. This is the only guarantee that we could survive beyond luck in a deceitful milieu. Our failure to do so could also lead to our premature death. This is the irrefutable truthfulness of the human species.

Men crave for independence. We long to be detached from our state of codependency. Sometimes, the weight of our existence incites the need for detachment in us. Other times, we want to express our individuality. But to do so, it must also be said, we often feel that we must be free.

The depressing fait accompli is that a mere want to be free is not enough to instill freedom in a person in its most unexciting sense. Sometimes, there is no freedom to be had. Accordingly, we invent our own. We create our own sense of freedom. However, our approach to what freedom is or what it could be often mirror our [own] fantasy as to how we perceive ourselves in the world of others.

It can be hard to survive in a world contrived to take away one's Beingness. It could be easier to let go of the self as a strategy to survive beyond luck. Perhaps the mere fact of having the capacity to let go of the self is a sign of freedom.

Life is a burden. Staying alive often requires the person to be a certain way. Yet, there can be no freedom in being a certain way. If being free means the person must be this way or that way, then he is not free to be. Freedom is always unconditional. Freedom is never relative to a particularity.

Being free is to be unconstrained. Being free is to be unrestricted. Being free is to be unabridged. Being free is to be unbound. Being free is to be sans restrictions; that is, be they collective or self-imposed.

When the person finds the self under restrictions, his existence becomes a load. When the person knows that he is not free, he seeks excuses to justify his inability to be free. As a result, life could easily become an insuperable struggle.

When a person realizes that he is living in a state of perpetual bondage, life could become dull and depressing for that individual. He might find the self in a constant strive to escape the grim reality, which he might be facing. But the search for freedom might as well become the search for a better life. The need to emancipate the self from the fact of life, which a person faces in his quotidian, might also allow that individual to discover his essence in the most tangible manner.

Constantly striving for freedom might become the only pursuit, which could provide a sense of purpose to an individual. This search might be the only reason that keeps him alive and well. This aim might be the reason that catapults the individual in the world. That calling might be the only motive that keeps the person going, even though life might be dull and depressing. That undertaking might become the catalyst of the individual's existence.

The problem is that few people understand the need to strive for their freedom. Here, I am not referring to freedom in the most trivial sense. I am referring to real freedom. That is, I am echoing the need for freedom of the mind, freedom of the soul, and even freedom of the body. That freedom, to say it again, is not real to the extent that it is tangible. In its place, it is the freedom of perception.

Hardly any of us understand the impact of preventing another from perceiving his [own] state of freedom. We are likely to abdicate our intrinsic inclination to daydream about ourselves to others. But this is not by coincidence.

We were taught [at an early age] to relinquish ourselves to others under the presumption that they know best. We are likely to become mental slaves. We cannot perceive any state of being where we are truly free, at least, in the mind. As a result, we could not perceive our freedom or any state of being similar to that independently.

Our inability to attain true freedom handicaps us. We often become useless creatures that roam the planet in the search of meaning. But meaning, if we ever found it, would be relegated to what others assign to themselves. In this case, what meaning is (or what it could be) is always inconsequential, for it would always be subjective. By contrast, it would not necessarily be the result of our own perception or subjectivity.

We are often lost in our search for meaning. We are condemned to strive for freedom, which, even if

Discourse on Human Freedom

we were to found it, would never be ours. We are condemned to be slaves, both in the body and in the mind.

Our perception of our own freedom is vital for our own existence. The foundation of our being depends on our capacity to distinguish it from that of others. But only some of us understand the need to preserve our Beingness in a restricted social place. Only a small number of us understand the need to strive to survive, at least, at all costs. Even fewer of us grasp that such a need could only derive from our perception of our state of being at any given point in time. We do not understand that our perception about freedom could only derive from our sense of being free to be whenever, however, or wherever we might want to be.

9

Searching for Freedom

A search for freedom could become a strategy to escape the load of life. If not, it could become an illusion, which, from our vantage point, might help soothe the calamity we face in our quotidian. Aiming for freedom could become a modus for survival. It could become a way to appease the bitterness of our living conditions.

Longing for freedom appeases our most primal fears. It is a way to reassure ourselves that everything is going to be all right. It provides us a sense of direction. It reinforces of our beliefs about our existence. It endows with us a sense of control over the self or an illusion of that.

Discourse on Human Freedom

When we think we are free, we might feel the weight of life lifted off our shoulders. Making out being free affords us a sense of relief. It helps us deal with the misfortunes of our existence. It helps us grasp our sense of precocity in a world in which we have little or no control. Aiming for freedom provides us with a sense of independence. It strengthens our notions (however misguided they might be) about our place in the universe. That feeling makes life easier to accept.

Our beliefs about freedom provide a sense of comfort; that is, however bogus such a sense might be. These convictions are likely to buttress our assumed detachment from everything that is human or from anything that could be human [or natural]. But we are aware that freedom, at least, the way we envisage it, is always hard to pin down. We know that it could never be otherwise. So, we strive to be free, at least, we tell ourselves that, while knowing that we will never achieve that feat.

Human freedom (or the perception thereof) is only a mirage in a desert. It is not real. At best, it is a make belief kernel. At worst, it is a dream, which we know will never come true.

Yes, we strive to be, while knowing that we will never be the way we imagine ourselves to be. This is the essence of our futility. This is also the essence of our quiddity. Moreover, this is the nature of any meaning, which we often assign to our actuality.

We dwell in vain in a futile search for meaning. We consider the search itself "freedom." But how could it be that way? How could we be free simply by wanting to be that way? We could not be free for the mere fact of trying to be free. Stating otherwise would be illogical; if not, making such a claim would be patently pompous. Yet, this is how we conceptualize our freedom. Is it not a tragedy?

Notwithstanding the above perspectives, I could not dismiss the human craving for freedom on the basis that such a state of being is unattainable. I could not deny the human passion to be free. I would not equate such a passion for freedom as a tangible state of freedom itself. Wanting to be free is not an indication of freedom in the most tangible sense. The freedom itself must be available. But this is not the case at all.

The unavailability of freedom itself does not invalidate its necessity. The search for freedom may lead to realities, which could heighten the need for freedom. Otherwise, it could undermine such a feat. In any case, the concept of freedom could have real-world consequences.

The freedom (or the lack thereof), which human beings crave for, could become a tangible state of being. It could reflect a transient state of the mind. Thus, the desire to be emancipated could inform the way the person behaves in his environment at a particular moment in time.

The more we try to emancipate ourselves from our perceived encroachments, the more enslaved we become. The more we try to free ourselves, the deeper we plunge in a web of invisible cages. This is the source of all human tragedies. This is our calamity, particularly when it comes to our search for freedom in places where such a search is improbable or even impractical.

When we are faced with that sordid fact, we often find ourselves in a state of desolation. At times, we live in despair. We abandon ourselves to our fate. We relinquish ourselves. Sometimes, it is because of our inability to make out our own freedom. Other times, we strive to survive. We live to tell our tale. We live with the hope that one day we will be free. But when we could not perceive our freedom or any chance of achieving it, our world could collapse. Even the whole world become devoid of hope. Life could become a depressing trial.

Immigrants often found out they could never be free on foreign lands. Apart from the implications of not being free, the prospects of never being free could unleash a veil of darkness in an immigrant's world. Being foreign in a new social milieu could complicate a person's existence. The individual could easily become invisible.

Let us see the specter of freedom from a practical slant. Let us assess the plight of immigrants. Let us examine the struggles of illegal aliens to claim their

freedom in America. But let us do so from a
philosophical cosmology.

10

Choice versus Freedom

Despite of the theoretical nature of the term freedom, there is a bit of tangibility to the notion. We could explore the concept from a practical lens. But let us do so from an immigrant's worldview

The questions worth asking here include the following: Are immigrants always free to be? Do they have a choice to be this way or that way on foreign lands? Could they decide whether to endure or else give up on themselves in a foreign milieu? Could they decide to return home at any point during their immigration journey?

Suppose that Patricia, a young woman from Honduras, left home in her teen years to immigrate elsewhere. At home, Patricia was living in a grim circumstance. After her parents passed away, she had no means of survival. Most young girls in Patricia's *barrio* were doing odd jobs to make ends meet. Some of them were working the streets at night. But the young woman had greater ambitions. She cherished the dream of moving to America.

Patricia left Honduras in the search of a better life. With little to no money, Patricia managed to move to Mexico. She ultimately found her way in the United States. She came to America in the hope of making a better life for herself.

Could we say that Patricia was seeking freedom when she left home? Could we say that she found that freedom when she arrived in the United States? Would Patricia ever know real freedom? Let us ponder on these questions as we move along.

Let us consider Marta. She is in her late thirties. She moved to the United States from Nicaragua. Presently, Marta lives in San Diego, California. But she has no legal documents to live in America. She should not be in the country.

Life is hard for this young woman. As an undocumented immigrant, Marta lives in hiding. She is afraid of immigration officials. She is constantly under stress. Marta dreads the possibility that she might be sent back to Nicaragua. Regardless of her situation, the young Marta does not want to leave America. She would rather live in infrahuman conditions on a foreign land rather than returning home to live in abject poverty.

Life is not rosy for Marta in America. Without the proper documents, she could not find work anywhere. She struggles to feed herself.

In spite of it all, Marta perseveres. Every day, she strives to survive. She does odd jobs to sustain herself. Could we say that Marta is free?

Let us consider the young Claudia. She is an undocumented immigrant from Guatemala. She has been living in America for seven years now.

Claudia met Ernesto; they fell in love. Ernesto is a legal U.S. resident. He is from Guatemala as well.

Discourse on Human Freedom

Ernesto promised to marry Claudia so she could regularize her immigration status. The problem is that Ernesto has a hot temper. He is a heavy drinker. Ernesto loves his *cervezas frias* (cold beers). When Ernesto is under the influence of alcohol, he can become violent. Although Ernesto and Claudia have a child together, life is miserable for Claudia. Ernesto can be abusive toward the young woman.

For Claudia, living with Ernesto is like living in hell. He assaults her constantly, most often, for no fault of her own. The ill treatments that Ernesto subjects Claudia can be verbal. They can be physical; they can be psychological.

Claudia would like to leave Ernesto. But she feels trapped in the relationship. Claudia is unsure that she would be able to provide for her child on her own. Therein lies her dilemma.

In Claudia's case, could we speak of freedom? Does Claudia have a choice to be a certain way? Let us consider another scenario, which could help us make sense of the inescapable verity immigrants often face on foreign lands.

Alonzo is a Mexican citizen. He came to the United States with a student visa. He studied from a prestigious university. For some reason, the young man could not find work anywhere. Should he return home?

Let us consider the young Joachim. He was born in Mexico. His parents crossed the border to the United States. They were searching for a better life for the little Joachim in America.

The young boy was six years old when he arrived in the United States. His parents never mentioned that he did not have legal papers to live in the country. When Joachim turned eighteen, the young man found out that he was undocumented. What could the young Joachim do? Should he return to Mexico?

What would you say about Felix? He was nineteen years old when he crossed the U.S./Mexico border. On Felix's arrival to the United States, border patrol agents detained him. They gave the young man two options. Either he returns to Mexico or he would be detained in an immigration

Discourse on Human Freedom

jail. Subsequently, they said, he will be deported. Does Felix have a real choice?

In the examples cited earlier, the protagonists found themselves in a predicament. On the one hand, they left home in the search of a better life. We could say that they were seeking freedom. Perhaps they were seeking economic freedom. But the life they found in America is not what they expected.

Should they take their reality in America as it is or should they get out of the country? Better yet, do they have the choice to leave America? If they decided not to leave, could we say that they exerted their freedom by accepting their new social reality? These are interesting questions. Few people could answer them objectively.

11

Freedom in the Real World

When we speak of human freedom, what do we mean? What are the practical implications of being free or being perceived that way? Could we consider an act or an omission as being an independent happening in a person's life? Could we say that an act or an omission expresses a person's freedom or the lack of that? What do we mean when we speak about freedom, at least, in the real world?

The thought of freedom is more complicated than most people realize. It is easier to say that so-and-so is free to be this way or that way. It is relatively easy to claim that so-and-so did this intentionally or he omitted the self from doing that willingly. Without regard of the circumstances a person might face, we seldom consider the circumstances of an act or the cause of an omission. We seldom consider the outside effects that instigated an act or an omission.

When we speak about freedom, we are likely to overlook the realities, which might hamper the state of being free itself. We are likely to neglect the actuality of that freedom or the view of that. We are always wrong when we speak about the freedom others supposedly know.

We do not have enough insights into the truth that others supposedly experience in their quotidian to make a clear deduction about their social reality. Therefore, we could not determine, at least, with certainty, whether they are free in the tangible sense or whether they are free [or could be free] in the mind. Simply put, we could not be certain that others see their freedom from a posture that resembles our own.

Taking into considerations the scenarios sketched earlier, it would be fanciful to claim that the protagonists enjoy any real freedom, for there were other circumstances, which could influence their choice or the illusion of that. These circumstances could hamper their view of their social problems. In view of that, individual perceptions about freedom, at least, in the previously noted instances, could not explain the extent of the veracity these people faced.

What I am saying is that I could not examine the story of these immigrants in a vacuum. I could not overlook the actuality of these characters with other social realities, which might or might not have been obvious to them. I could not undermine the political circumstances that led them to leave their land. I could not overstate the psychological ramifications of these events. I could not ignore the societal implications of their accomplishments during their crucibles or the lack of that. Thus, I could not speak about freedom as a stand-alone actuality when examining the reality these individuals faced on foreign lands.

The mental picture we often hold about freedom epitomizes the presumption that every individual is already detached from his natural environment. Whatever the person does is a choice, which is solely based on that individual's assessment of his social conditions. By that logic, some people might say that the person is always responsible for any act [or any omission]. The individual would also be responsible for any choice either taken or omitted. Failure to do so, some people might argue, would show individual freedom at the most mechanic level. But would that be an infallible truth? I would say not all. In fact, I disagree—fervently, I must say—with the previous understandings.

I would contend that every action [or omission] is a direct response to a reality, which the person did not necessarily engender. Any response, be it an action or an omission, in turn, could be a reaction to another action, which may or may not concern the person who takes that action directly or indirectly or the person who admits that action openly or in some way. It may not even be related to the individual who started the original action.

Here at least, we must grasp the nature of the codependency, which the individual entertains with the environment where he evolves. It does not matter whether that person engaged in a conduct or omitted to do the same consciously or unconsciously. It does not matter whether the person did so (or failed to do so) in a particular turf. We must understand the agency that might have engendered the action or the omission in the first place.

In every facet of a social milieu, antics about freedom are always illusory. A society, in its most fundamental organization, relies on a constant dependency among its members. So long as you leave in a social space, you could never be on your own [or independent]. There, you could never enjoy a state of liberation that is independent of what the milieu itself would allow. You could not be without restrictions. You could not be without constraints. As such, you could never escape the grip the environment has on you. From here, you could never be free, at least, if you were to be held responsible for your actions or your omissions.

We could agree to disagree that every human being is a survivalist. While we are not always aware of our innate want to survive, we often come to that realization at some point in our lives or even before we die. Does that mean that we are always free to be? I would say no.

Could we say that the individual at all times plays a role in his [own] success or even in his [own] destruction? If so, to what extent could we hold ourselves responsible for our misfortunes in a locale, which others designed for us? Let us examine these questions from the viewpoint of an existentialist.

12

An Existentialist Approach to Freedom

An existentialist, notably a person in the caliber of Jean-Paul Sartre, often speaks of human freedom pompously. It is as if such a way of being could be the crowning jewel of life or human existence itself. The understanding here is that every human being has to strive for freedom.

Modern existential idealists often project intellectual shenanigans about human freedom. These thinkers often take the perception to a higher level. They often take the chimera of being free too seriously, if you ask me. Freedom, from my vantage point, is not a *mere will* to be. It is not a *measly desire* to be one way or another.

From an existentialist paradigm, every human being is free to be whenever, however, and for whatever the reason might be. Here of course, I propose to debate the craze about freedom from a different standpoint.

From an existentialist worldview, freedom affords the person the means to strive to survive. The person would be in control of his past. He could shape his present. He could map out his future. Thus, by looking at the term freedom from an existentialist acumen, one might say that being free is a supreme sign of existence. It shows independence in the face of both natural and unnatural encroachments.

From an existentialist lens, when the person is free, he is completely detached from anything or from anyone else. The person is in charge of his world. But that view, I would argue, is illogical.

This approach to human ontology suggests that there is only one state of freedom in the world of men. It is the state of being free itself. The problem

Ben Wood Johnson

is that it is not clear whether the freedom existentialists speak of is tangible, abstract, or both.

When existentialist speak of freedom, what are they talking about, really? Are they talking about the actuality that people are experiencing at a given point in time? Is it the freedom of the mind? Is it the freedom of the body? Is it complete freedom?

Suppose the freedom itself is tangible, once a state of being free has been achieved, could we say that the person is going to be free forever? Could we say the person would never need to be free in a specific situation? Modern existentialists would answer yes to these questions. But their approach, at least, in my view, would be illogical. The fad of freedom, at least, the way contemporary existentialists see it, does not match with the real world.

Freedom is merely a facet of being. Freedom, at least, as humans conceive the insight, is only relevant when there is a need for it. Such a need always depends on the entity that needs the freedom in the first place. It also depends on the entity that seeks to deprive others of their freedom.

In a man's world, there is always a need for freedom from someone. There is always a need for freedom from something. The question worthy of note here is whether freedom is always achievable in similar places.

It is important to realize the extent of freedom in society. It is necessary to become accustomed to our natural inclinations to be a certain way. It is of utmost importance to understand that there is a constant need to deprive others of their freedom. What could explain that reality, you might ask? The answer is that we could not be free all at once. This is the nature of being in the world.

No one could be free unless the individual who needs such freedom was already deprived of such a way of being. Freedom, if it existed at all, would be a short-lived state of being. To echo a previous understanding, I would say that there is no such a state in the most tangible sense in society. No one is free in a social ambience. Freedom would defeat society in its most foundational state. Let me explain why...

13

An Independent State of Mind

While I proclaim there is no freedom in a social ambient, most modern existentialists could argue to the contrary. Yet, an existentialist means of analysis about human encroachments [or the lack thereof] offers little or no guideline to grasping the need for freedom. This would be true even if we were to examine the frivolity of the term freedom in its most fundamental sense or in its most epistemological, if not elementary, sense. It would not be capricious to say that the freedom, which existentialists often speak of, is a stand-alone state of being that men experience in their world.

Discourse on Human Freedom

While in the ontological sense, freedom could be understood as an independent state of mind, the same could not be said when we are talking about a social locale. The foundation of every social environ is co-dependency. Thus, talking about freedom in such an environment is intellectually dishonest. It would be mute to assess the nature of human ontology in a social vacuum.

Speaking of freedom as if it were a primary goal in human existence would be a misguided racket. Doing so would not allow us to understand the nature of human suffering. First, we must grasp what might induce a man to strive for freedom. We must also cater the genesis (or the reasons), which might impede such a thirst for freedom.

Every society is unjust. But a state of oppression is always antithetic to the caprice of freedom. This is so at the core meaning of the term. For these considerations, there can be no freedom, for the creation of every society resulted from oppression, be it consented or imposed.

The need for freedom, at least, at first, is always a social matter. Freedom in a social sphere is seldom an ontological issue. It is not up to the person to be free. It is up to society to create the conditions for the person not to need freedom in the first place. But the individual may never realize such a need, even on the face of his calamities unless society reveals it to him. Hence, there can be no freedom in a social circle, for the mania about being free or the craving for such a state of being is invariably contrary to the existence of society itself.

My point is that it would not suit society if every person were to be free. This is the case even in the most theoretical sense of the word "Freedom." The social locus where we evolve is an unavoidable labyrinth. That is why—I would say—it is always important to explore the social causes, which may affect the need for survival, as a result, which may feign the need for freedom.

To restate an earlier understanding, freedom is only necessary when it is unavailable. It is important to comprehend the determinant factor for which there might be a need for freedom before understanding what freedom is or what it could be. Speaking about freedom in a co-dependent environment as if it were an independent state of being is false-hearted.

The freedom that modern existentialists often speak of is only real to the extent that society or the social milieu makes it possible. The problem is that such a state of being is always contradictory to the existence of society itself. In it, lies a fundamental contradiction in the perverseness of freedom within a social backdrop.

14

Why You Must be Free

Human beings are free only when they could see [or when they could construe] such a need. But to arrive at a state where the need for freedom is obvious, the person must be able to reflect on the state of the self at the most intrinsic state. The person must be able to examine the self in the environment where he finds the self. All right, this is not always possible. This might not even be feasible. Too many diversions often hold the person captive both mentally and physically.

The person is often lost in his social crucibles. He is neglected; he is left to fend for himself. Or else, the person has to deal with his social plights. He seldom succeeds in this endeavor though.

The person might put out of the mind the need to survive. While the person might fail to remember his priorities to survive, he might not realize the need to be free. The person might become moribund. The person might become the subject of his social circumstances. The person might forget to be free, for, in his mind, he might not see the need for such a way of being.

Freedom could also be a death sentence. In this case, the person might see his freedom as a burden. The person might not want to be free. Similarly, he might not want others to be free.

Under a similar regimen, the person could ask to be held in captivity. The person might even concoct a plan to keep not only the self in seclusion, but also others in a state of prolonged confinement. The person could feel the need to be in prison as a way to be free. From the person's vantage point, he prefers to be in bondage instead of letting others be free, for their freedom could be a threat to his own Beingness. From the person's eyehole as well, if others were free, that could be an impediment to his state of captivity, which, in turn, could affect his perceived sense of freedom. This is the absurdum of human freedom or the search for it.

We saw a similar happening during the Covid-19 outbreak. Countless people were on the side of confinement. Many thought that staying at home during the pandemic was the right thing to do. For many people, it made sense to take away the freedom of the individual to be a certain way. It was fascinating to hear [or to see] those who often portrayed themselves as freedom lovers asking their government to imprison everyone in the name of freedom.

When the person evolves in a continual state of bondage (whether such a state is mental or physical), he could not see the need to be free. The person might forego the need to survive if he were not able to perceive an immediate threat to that survival. From here, the person might try to keep his condition as is, for it might suit him well.

The person might strive to keep his Beingness as is, for it would undermine that of others. The person might strive relentlessly to be [or to remain] in oppression, for he could not perceive himself as being oppressed. This is the tragedy of being in self-bondage. The coronavirus pandemic illustrated that truism with a poignant panorama.

Under such a calamitous state, the person might feel the need to forego the self in finding the means to survive serendipitously. He might prevent others from surviving beyond chance. The person might also lack the introspective dexterity to save the self from the self or from the social encroachments, which he might be facing. By contrast, the person might become an instigator of pain and suffering for others. In any case, you must be free or you must find a way to be that way.

15

Advocating for Self-Confinement

During the peak of the coronavirus pandemic, I made an interesting social experiment. In the United States, I observed two types of individuals who did not mind being deprived of their freedom or the illusion thereof. It was fascinating to watch.

There were those who saw nothing wrong in the confinement itself. They saw it as a compromise for the greater good. These people were likely to demand more actions from the government to stop the spread of the disease. Conversely, there were those who, not only did not mind the confinement, but also were likely to require that others accept it.

These individuals promoted the confinement to a point where they enforced it themselves. In many cases, they did so zealously.

Some people espoused a mob mentality against those who viewed the spread of the virus differently. These individuals were likely to shun, and, in most cases, outcast, those who opposed government actions. It was as if these people wanted, not only themselves to be in confinement, but also anyone else.

As I observed this incongruity in my locality, I wondered what might incite a person to ask to be deprived of his freedom. I realized that in the two mentioned groups, there were a few interesting patterns, which are worthy of further analysis. Agreed, my assessment here is not scientific by any means. It is worth noting nonetheless.

Anyway, it appeared that those who saw nothing wrong in the confinement were likely well placed within the social stratum. That is, many of these individuals appeared to live a decent life; that is, they lived comfortably. Freedom, to put it like that, was ostensibly the least of their worries. These people appeared well grounded in their social milieu.

On the other side of the coin, those who, not only saw nothing wrong in the confinement, but also wanted it to be as pervasive as possible, were on an even higher social scale. These people seemed well grounded in their social milieu. They also seemed comfortable financially. But they also appeared motivated to support or to refute the confinement for other reasons. Many people had a political motive to advocate for the confinement of both the self and others.

There were those who opposed the confinement. But they did so not only for political, but also for economic interests. In the United States, the coronavirus epidemic occurred during an election year. Most Americans had political incentives either to favor or to oppose the confinement.

While I will not delve in the political organ or even the economic facet of the confinement, a third group is worth outlining here. These individuals were cautious about the hysteria of confinement. They had good reasons to feel that way.

For these people, the confinement was akin to a death sentence. For many of them, there was no difference between dying of the virus and dying of economic starvation. For these people, their livelihood depended on their capacity to move about. From their vantage point, the confinement was not good for their survival.

Not to stray away from the purpose of this discussion, let me point out this work is not about the Covid-19 in itself. It is not even about the licentious policies that guided the global response to the pandemic. But it is equally important to echo the greater issue at hand. In this instance, it is our analysis about the scope of human freedom.

As I sought to articulate in previous paragraphs, the coronavirus illustrated the degree to which humans enjoy little or no freedom. By contrast, a human aspiration to freedom is what keeps us sane in the face of our seclusion, be it mental or physical. The problem is that in certain circumstances, even our capacity to imagine our freedom is impossible. This grim reality often happens to immigrants, particularly when they arrive on foreign lands. This is so, at least, in the beginning of their journey away from the homeland.

The immigrant has to find the means to save the self. However, the person must do so amid the most difficult moments of his life. The person must free the self against all odds. No matter what, the immigrant must pull through. Still, the immigrant must do so in his own term or his own way. The tragedy is that this is not always feasible.

The immigrant often feels trapped in his new social locale. This actuality epitomizes the calamity of being foreign in a milieu designed by others and for others. The person may find the self in a disadvantageous situation. He might not be able to carry on; he might not be able to survive on his own.

The person might find it necessary, if not urgent, to familiarize the self with the reality, which others have always known. But it always ends in a tragedy. The person is sure to fail in his attempt to secure a better living experience for himself and for others. Most often, there is no way out. The person is trapped.

The immigrant could not return home, for he left that place in the search of a better life. However, the person could not always live under the circumstances that he might be forced to exist. Then, the search for freedom might become an unattainable pursuit, which, in turn, might keep the person alive.

What is it that the immigrant could do under similar circumstances? I would not know what to tell you. Whilst the immigrant wants to survive, that survival might be impossible. The freedom to be this way or that way is always beyond his reach.

In the midst of it all, I would say, the immigrant must understand his reality. He must adjust the self to that actuality. The problem is that, to do so—I would also argue—the person, in this case, the immigrant, must reflect on the self. Thus, the person or the immigrant (whatever the case may be) must philosophize. In doing so, the individual would be able to construe his freedom or any sense thereof.

You might be asking, what do I mean by philosophizing? I will not delve in the crux of this question. I addressed it in a previous work. Please see the book titled *Cogito, Ergo Philosophus* to learn more. Let us say that the term philosophy implies a person's capacity to see the world for what it is and not how others project it to him. But such a capacity is not innate.

The person must develop that introspective capability on his own, for his own, with his own, and for his own sake. In it lies the dichotomy of wanting to be free and being able to be free. In it lies the infeasibility of freedom and the incongruity of wanting to remain in captivity. All the same, in it lies the magnanimity of freedom or the illusion of that.

Discourse on Human Freedom

16

A Change of Mindset

When I was in secondary school (high school), I learned that philosophy, and ordinary life intertwined. I remember refuting that argument zealously. But I got embroiled in a heated debate with some of my classmates. We did not agree about the essence of the term philosophy.

Many of my friends argued that every facet of life could be examined through a philosophical discernment. I refused to drink this cup of bitter tea. I rejected this velleity passionately. It sounded like a shrouded approval of an intellectual psychosis. I did not want to take part of that misguided approach to an important concept. I did not hide that viewpoint though.

I made it clear to my classmates that I did not think that philosophy could be approached from a *Terre-à-Terre* (or from a trivial) standpoint. A few of my friends were repulsed by my refusal to open my mind to an unpleasant fact, which almost all of us had been witnessing in our daily rituals. They repudiated me as someone who is pushing an aristocratic view of the world. Of course, I did not see myself under such a prism.

Life is not always "Champagne and Caviar," someone echoed. Philosophy is not what comes out of the so-called "factories of knowledge" or from prestigious universities, someone else pointed out. A few of my classmates argued that these places are driven by a desire to imprison the person in the mind by inculcating him notions that do not reflect the world itself. Such an approach to the real world, I retorted, is not only pompous, but it is also demeaning to the corporeality others face in their quotidian.

It did not take much for me to have a change of outlook. After a deeper scrutiny of my life and the lives of those around me, I found it necessary to amend my beliefs about philosophy. I realized that I was the living proof that philosophy and ordinary life intertwine. I also realized that this was the case in the most basic sense of the term philosophy.

During that period, I lived in a squalid social milieu. I was a prisoner in that decaying hub. My grandmother grew up in that environment. My mother grew up in it. I was also poised to becoming a part of that dreadful locus. There, poverty was the inescapable norm. There was no exception.

While everyone I knew in my neighborhood was poor, no one accepted his or her state of decrepitude. Everyone was seeking a strategy, which would allow him or her to get out of that social labyrinth. Many were trying [arduously, to say the least] to emancipate the self from this awful social imbroglio. Some of them sought a way out, while trying to maintain a footing in the milieu.

Everyone I knew in my neighborhood wanted to survive. Indeed, most people were surviving. But only a few were certain of their tomorrow. Only a few had a long-term plan for survival. The rest of them lived on a day-to-day basis. While they were surviving, they could only do so serendipitously. As I witnessed that depressing social tangibility, I did not want to end up like my neighbors. I wanted to emancipate myself from the awful social materialization that awaited me. I was looking for a way out of my social actuality. I wanted to survive beyond luck.

I saw my education as my ticket to economic freedom. Being erudite, I thought, was my only way out of my everlasting situation of poverty. As I grew older, I realized that my life was incumbent on my grasping of the social arena itself.

To my surprise, I found out that my education had little [or nothing] to do with my survival. I realized that a need to be free and my capacity to be that way intersected. That intersection, in turn, provided me freedom or a sense of that state of being. I realized that I had a role to play in my destiny.

Whilst I was a captive of my putrid social decor, I concluded that I could create a means to escape it, albeit superficially. I realized that I could be free or I could say to myself that I am that way.

I concluded that the only way to arrive at that state (or the perception of that) was for me to philosophize. This was the only way, I thought, for a person who dwells in captivity to be free. If not, it is a way to experience such a state of the mind.

Yes, I have been philosophizing all along. I have been seeking freedom all along. Okay, whether I have been truly free is a different debate, which I would prefer to put aside for another conversation. I would admit that I have constantly been on a quest for freedom. As such, I have always been a philosopher. Only, I never saw myself in such a way.

I agree with my classmates now. Human survival, freedom, and the capacity to ponder about the reality of the self intersect. If you could think, you could emancipate the self from any encroachment so imposed or so superposed. Certainly, that does not mean that you would be free. All it means is that you could create your own sense of freedom in a state of perpetual bondage.

17

Born to be a Prisoner

Most people exist only to be enslaved. They enjoy being deprived of any sense of autonomy because they never had it. They do not know what it means to be free or to feel free.

Seclusion often becomes a way of life for these individuals. They could not be themselves, unless they are under the purview of others. They could not be free, unless they are told that they are free.

There is an absurd dependency between the individual and the collective. Most societies were designed to reflect that reality. Most environments were designed to entice the individual. These places could only exist so long as the person could not.

Discourse on Human Freedom

Social obstacles are designed to imprison the person, not only in his soul, but also in his body. Most social rules are designed to capture the person in his physical self. That is the reason, which might explain why incarceration is the preferred form of punishment, particularly for those who dare to disobey social rules. That is the reason as well social deprivation is a preferred means of punishment for those who dare to dream of their emancipation. But there is nothing wrong in striving to be you.

If you allowed your problems to become a part of your existence, you would live in a state of bondage forever. If you could survive in the face of your calamities, then you could also know freedom; if not, you could experiment something akin to that. This is the essence of your plights in this world. You must find a way to be, even though it might be improbable or impossible.

Life and philosophy are intricately similar. Survival depends on the person's capacity to ponder.[3] In doing so, the person would know that

---

[3] Please see the book titled *"Cogito, Ergo Philosophus"* to learn more about that understanding.

he is not free. The person would behave that way. I have held this view so dear I have become a fervent proponent of this intellectual conception.

The search for freedom is the story of humanity. The sad truth is that we live in an existential maze. As an immigrant, however, I am constantly aware of my being. I know that I am stuck in my reality.

I am conscious that I could not leave the unhealthy place, which typifies my grim social conditions. Every day, I strive to survive. I accept my veracity. I immolate myself. I learn to endure. I learn to be according to the way others want me to be. And so, I humble myself before my inescapable destiny in a world I could not dare change.

Does that mean that I am free to leave, but I refuse to do so? Does that mean that I am free at my core being because I accept my new social reality? I would say so. Granted, modern existentialists would probably say yes on my behalf. Nonetheless, they would be mistaken about my reality.

At a young age, I left my home. I immigrated to America. Since my arrival on this foreign land, my life has been difficult. To cope, I have resorted to many strategies. I have done it all in an attempt to survive. In the midst of my calamities, I often reflect on my life circumstances. I persistently adjust to my social whereabouts. I endure; I persevere in my desire to survive. But I will continue to strive. I will survive until the end of my time.

Being an immigrant is a tragedy for many of us. In essence, we cannot enjoy freedom or any sense of that. We could not claim to be free, for our existence is relative to the realities of our social latitude. Besides, if we were to allow ourselves to fall on the wrong path, we could lose our essence.

We know that we are not free. We know that we could not be the way we might want to be. We know that we could not dare to be the way we might want to be. Simply put, we could not save ourselves from our reality.

Most immigrants live in a state of mental prison. They dwell in a state of physical and economic bondage. Despite that, they strive, constantly at times, to emancipate themselves from that grim situation. They live with hopes. They have learned to accept their reality.

Would immigrants ever succeed beyond chance on foreign lands? Even if they were to make it, would it last? Answers are inevitably subjective. Put differently, only you could gauge your level of success in this regard. Only you could determine whether you are free to be. Only you could live with the burden of wanting to be free. Therefore, you need to decide whether you *need* freedom or whether you *want* to experience that state of being as a way to emancipate yourself from a putrid social reality. In any case, only you must concretize the actuality that you face in your quotidian. Thus, achieving freedom (or the illusion of that) is always a personal undertaken.

At this point in the manuscript, let us reconsider a few of the questions posed earlier. Taking into account some of the claims echoed in this text thus far, would you say that you are always free to be no matter how you might want to be at any given point, time, and place? Even during the coronavirus pandemic, would you say that you are free?

For the sake of the arguments, let us say that you are not free in any way, shape, or form. Do you think that you could emancipate yourself from your encroachments, be they social, mental, or physical? Could you rid yourself of the emprise of your social milieu on your Beingness? Could you be you simply for being who you are? Could you be you beyond the expectations of the collective?

This is not to belabor the point. But let us say that you recognize that you are indeed a captive of your social milieu. Could you be free in the mind? Could you rid yourself of your mental state of perpetual seclusion? Is there a freedom to be had and all you have to do is reach for it? Could you be free (be it in the flesh or in the mind)?

Now, I challenge you to answer any of the previous questions in the affirmative. That is to say, there is no freedom to be had on this stone called earth. That being said, you might chose to remain in bad faith. You may claim that you are free. You may even persuade yourself that others are free. But would that make it so in the most tangible sense? Would that be an indication of your freedom? I would say not at all.

18

The Importance of Philosophizing

A ny choice, so imposed or so superposed, is an obligation. Therefore, there is no way to be other than selecting one of the options so presented. In doing so, the option not selected is also a choice. Put differently, if a choice is *to be* or *not to be*, then any penchant, be it an action or an omission, could not be a sign of freedom. Rather, it would be a materialization of your captivity or you incapacity to be free.

I reckon that you might be able to achieve a sense of your own state of freedom. You might even do so in the face of an obligation, so imposed or so superposed. But that perception, in and of itself, would always be an illusion, for it could only be a subjective interpretation of a particular reality, which might not reflect your actuality. In any case, I could not construe your sense of freedom for you. In fact, no one could. That is why I could only let you be the judge and the jury of your own actuality.

What I am saying is that when it comes to my own freedom [or the sense thereof] in the most abstract intellect, I understand my limits. As well, I understand my possibilities or the lack thereof. Nonetheless, I know that I am not free in the intrinsic sense. Likewise, I know that when it comes to your freedom (that is, real or surreal), only you could construe it. Hence, I recognize that I have no clue.

I could not make any inferences about your perception of your actuality. I could not pretend to comprehend your rationality. Accordingly, when it comes to freedom in the most tangible sense, I must recognize that I have no clue, even for my own sake. But that does not mean that we could not dream about freedom. That does not mean we could not pursue such a state of being.

The question becomes; how could we perceive our own reality? What role that perception could play in helping us develop our freedom (be it real or perceived)? In these instances, there is only one answer. That is, we must philosophize.

Philosophy, I often echo, is the story of human beings in all their glory or in all their flaws. It is a story told from the prism of the person who is experiencing it. Philosophy is the only sustainable means for the person to understand his essence within the social vicinity where he evolves. It is a gateway to get a good grasp of the tangible world. It is the only path to freedom or a similar illusion.

The story of immigration speaks to all of us. It is the story of those of us who live away from our natural environment. It is the story of immigrants all over the globe.

I have lived instances that could only be toxic for my Beingness. It is true that my suffering might not be obvious to someone else. Such instances could only be made out in the introspective realm. Only I could assess my own materiality in the world. Only I could sense my tribulations. Only I could be me. Thus, my freedom, or any sense of that, could only dwell in my mind.

Assessing my actuality in the most tangible sense could only be possible in the mind; my own mind, that is. Assessing my freedom in the same manner would only be possible through the philosophical realm. What is a state of anguish to one person, another would always perceive it differently, for what is suffering for one individual would always be a different experience for someone else. Thus, what is pain to one person another would always make it out in a different way.

My point is that leaving one's environment for another place (or for another social ambience at that) is not always easy. It takes guts to wake up one day and leave one's familiar circumstances. This is often the case no matter how soiled such a reality might be or no matter how degrading such a way of being might be. It is difficult to uproot oneself from one place to go somewhere else. It takes a man to save another, even though that man might be oneself.

I admit it here as well; saving oneself is not that easy. Few could do it; few could save their own selves. Being free or sensing one's state of being that way makes no difference. In the face of the calamities one faces in this world, being free or feeling free may have no tangible meaning for the person. Failure to understand that materiality could lead to one's premature death.

As a person living miles away from the homeland, I know that I am not free. I make myself no illusions in this regard. Perhaps this is why I could not save myself from my own existential extinction. It is not for a lack of trying though.

Perhaps I am a coward. Perhaps I am practical. There is also the possibility that I might be attuned to my existence more than you think. I might be wiser than you know. But I may never know.

While I recognize that I am not free, I am not about to accept my circumstances without fighting back. I am considering alternatives. Only, my existence has not been cornered to a point where I feel that I have nothing to lose by parting from my unhappiness. I have a lot to lose. I am also aware of that struggle.

What is irrefutable is that I am tied up in my social locale. For a fact, I am in a mental prison. As a result, I cannot run away from my plight as easily as it might appear to you. I am not alone in my quandary. Many immigrants are experiencing a similar reality. This is the tragedy of being in a mental cage on a foreign social thrust.

19

Freedom as a Futile Endeavor

Most people cannot free themselves from their realities for panoply of reasons. Sometimes, there are loved ones, which might make it difficult for a person to leave a place, which might be extinguishing life out of him. Hence, there can be no way to free the self from the milieu where one finds the self. To that extent, there could be no freedom to be had under similar circumstances.

A person could not always leave memories behind in the search for a better life for oneself amid the misgivings that one faces. To say it again, it takes a man to save another. The sad truth is that most of us are not strong enough (or man enough) or attuned to our social environment to a point where we can understand the responsibility of preserving our own life.

We do not always realize that we have an obligation to live our life in its fullest. Faced with hardships, most of us are likely to ignore our intrinsic leaning to survive. But to survive, I would echo, we must do whatever our instincts tell us to do. What our guts tell us is usually the right course of action to take. But most often, I must also admit, we have to convince ourselves of that state of being.

Many of us have faced realities that required us to philosophize. No holds barred, we seldom did so. Some of us are prone to blame anyone but ourselves for our misfortunes. Does that mean we are free to the extent that others are also free? I would say no. To say it again, freedom [or the perception of that] is personal.

Others are prone to blame the self for their trials. We punish ourselves. We engage in self-destructions, be it physical or psychological. We are likely to victimize ourselves for being victimized. Is that a good strategy? Is that a sign of freedom? I would say no.

Despite our grim quiddity, hurting oneself may not be the best way to deal with our problems. While I may perceive my freedom to be a certain way, I could not blame the world for my woes. I could not blame others for my misfortunes as an immigrant. I also refuse to blame myself. The same, I refuse to hate others for my calamities on their land.

I understand my precocity as an immigrant. I make myself no illusion about the possibility that my life might be better elsewhere. This is the essence of my freedom. I refuse to be according to the way my social milieu wants me to be. I refuse to allow myself to become anything but myself. If freedom I have, it would be the freedom to remain true to my nature.

Notwithstanding my actuality, I will never hate those who hate me. I will never become like those who dedicated themselves to denying my freedom or the sense of that. I would not be like those who do not want to let me be. I could not hold a grudge against those who denied me a place to be me.

I could never be like those who rebuked me for seeking a better life on their lands. They too are experiencing the same mental bondage that I am facing. We are in the same economic prison. We are in the same rotting social situation. We are experiencing the same sordid collective reality.

In the most tangible sense of the term freedom, we are not free. We will never be that way. But that does not mean that the search for freedom is a futile endeavor. Instead, it is the essence of our survival.

20

My Philosophical Maturity

Since my high school experiment, I have developed an existential dependency over my capacity to philosophize. I continually reflect on myself. I constantly examine the demeanor of the people around me. Every moment of my life, I am thinking about ways to improve my existence. I come up with strategies for my long-term survival. I am attuned to my subsistence in ways that I never thought possible before.

I am aware of myself. I am aware of the actions that others take or make around me. I am aware of the actions that others omit, either by design or by inadvertence, around me. I am wary of what they do [or do not do] to me. I am attuned to what they do [or what they omit], which might affect me negatively.

Over the years, I have learned to become one with my nature. I realized that I have always been part of the cosmos. If God there is, he, she, or it is part of me, for I am a part of him, her, or it. I always take the everyday life [or the mundane] seriously. I have found my inner strength.

Amid the misery of life, most immigrants will discover that their inner strength was more powerful than they thought. As well, amid my social labyrinth, I realized that I have always had the power to shape my destiny, though I am not sure that I could drastically change my fate in the world of others. I venture day-by-day to change my reality. Within my limits, I do so whenever I feel like I could succeed in that endeavor.

As I grew older and became more mature, I realized that I am not the only person who could reflect on his life circumstances. This is so in the most fundamental sense of the word "Cogitating."

Ben Wood Johnson

Just as I can see my actuality in my world, others witness their reality from the same perspective. That being said, I have my [own] subjectivity about my state of freedom. I am sure that you have your own as well. In that case, I do not expect mine to be compatible with yours. You should have similar expectations.

Discourse on Human Freedom

Afterword

Throughout this work, I wanted to outline practical implications about freedom. I sought to explore the ramifications of being free [or not being that way under any circumstance]. It was important to examine the effects of human freedom [or the lack thereof], which are practical in nature. Tangentially, the text sought to relate the struggles immigrant families often face, as they endeavor, relentlessly at times, to adjust in a foreign locality.

To accomplish these goals, I proposed a simplistic approach. Perhaps this is the best way to understand irrationalities about human freedom. I examined the concept from an unsophisticated mindset. In doing so, I proposed a down-to-earth approach to the intellection of human freedom.

I wanted to bring a fresh perspective in the conversation. Throughout this manuscript as well, I questioned presuppositions about the nature of human freedom. Unequivocally, I rejected the view, which endorses that human beings are always free or they are always free to be.

The search for freedom is often interlaced with the search for meaning. But the extent to which a person's need to find the means to survive could yield tangible results is not clear. Linking human freedom with the search for meaning could lead to a dead-end. These concepts are not necessarily interlaced.

In spite of the previous concessions, the search for freedom could be both a futile quest and an indispensable undertaken, which the person must reconcile at some point. In doing so, he or she might develop of good sense of the self in the world. Perhaps in discovering the self, the person might find the self in the midst of the calamity, which the self must endure as a precondition to be free or to perceive such a state of being.

In this book as well, I sought to examine the degree to which freedom, or the view of that, is something that an ordinary man could make out, conceive, or perceive on his own. From a unique perspective, I sought to explain the degree to which human freedom intertwines with existing means to survive outside serendipity in a serendipitous world. The conclusion is irrefutably demoralizing. That is, there is no freedom to be had.

In any case, the being must strive to exist. He must subsist. However, the capacity to strive or the ability to survive, in and of itself, could not be freedom in the most tangible sense.

In sum, I offered a *Terre-à-Terre* approach in the debate. Vice versa, it was important to make my point as judiciously as possible. If you are still distorted about the views expressed here, I encourage you to see my other works about the telltale of human freedom.

Keep in mind that my approach to human freedom is simple. From my vantage point, freedom is not of this world. In whatever way, I reckon that being able to recognize that unpleasant state of being would make it possible for the individual to concretize his own reality in a world designed to capture his existence. But that concretization could make it possible as well for the person *to be* beyond chance. If you want to construe that conjecture as freedom, you are free to do so.

Index

Discourse on Human Freedom

Discourse on Human Freedom

About the Author

BEN WOOD JOHNSON, Ph.D.

Dr. Johnson is a social observer, a philosopher, and a multidisciplinary scholar. He writes about law, legal theory, education, public policy, politics, race and crime, and ethics.

Dr. Johnson graduated from Penn State University and Villanova University. He holds a Doctorate in Educational Leadership, a Master's degree in Political Science, a Master's degree in Public Administration, and a Bachelor's degree in Criminal Justice.

Dr. Johnson worked in law enforcement. He attended John Jay College of Criminal Justice. Dr. Johnson is fluent in several languages, including French, Spanish, Portuguese, and Italian.

Dr. Johnson enjoys reading, poetry, painting, and music. You may contact Dr. Ben Wood Johnson by e-mail. You may also reach him via the postal services. For other means of communication, see the information listed below.

Mailing Address

Eduka Solutions
330 W. Main St #214
Middletown, PA 17057

Email

E-mail Address: tkpubhouse@gmail.com

Social Media

Find Dr. Ben Wood Johnson on the following media platforms.

Twitter: @benwoodpost
Facebook: @benwoodpost

You may find Dr. Ben Wood Johnson on other online platforms, including his official blog site at www.benwoodpost.org. You may visit his website at www.benwoodjohnson.com. If you would like to learn more about Dr. Johnson's works, you may find them on his official bookstore at www.benwoodjbooks.com.

TESKO PUBLISHING
An independent publishing house

Discourse on Human Freedom

Other Works

Selected works by Dr. Ben Wood Johnson

1. Racism: What is it?

2. Sartrean Ethics: A Defense of Jean-Paul Sartre as a Moral Philosopher

3. Jean-Paul Sartre and Morality: A Legacy Under Attack

4. Sartre Lives On

5. Forced Out of Vietnam: A Policy Analysis of the Fall of Saigon

6. Natural Law: Morality and Obedience

7. Cogito Ergo Philosophus

8. Le Racisme et le Socialisme: La
   Discrimination Raciale dans un Milieu
   Capitaliste

9. International Law: The Rise of Russia as a
   Global Threat

10. Citizen Obedience: The Nature of Legal
    Obligation

11. Jean-Jacques Rousseau: A Collection of Short
    Essays

12. Être Noir : Quel Malheur !

13. L'homme et le Racisme: Être Responsable de
    vos Actions et Omissions

14. Pennsylvania Inspired Leadership: A
    Roadmap for American Educators

15. Adult Education in America: A Policy
    Assessment of Adult Learning

16. Striving to Survive: The Human Migration Story

17. Postcolonial Africa: Three Comparative Essays about the African State

18. Surviving the Coronavirus

19. Go Back Where You Came From

TESKO PUBLISHING

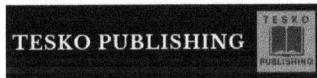

You may find other works by Dr. Ben Wood Johnson by visiting his blog.

MY EDUKA SOLUTIONS

BEN WOOD POST

www.benwoodpost.org

TESKO **PUBLISHING**
An independent publishing house

www.teskopublishing.com

Discourse on Human Freedom

www.ingramcontent.com/pod-product-compliance
Lightning Source LLC
LaVergne TN
LVHW011333080426
835513LV00006B/319